Studies

in

1 Timothy

Michael Penny

ISBN: 978-1-78364-521-3

www.obt.org.uk

****

The Open Bible Trust
Fordland Mount, Upper Basildon,
Reading, RG8 8LU, UK.

Studies in 1 Timothy

Contents

Page

Timothy: The Man

Timothy: The Man[1]

It seems that Timothy was around when Paul visited Lystra on his first missionary journey (Acts 14:8-20). That may have been the time when he came to believe in Christ as Paul refers to him as "my true son in the faith" (1 Timothy 1:2). By the time Paul visited Lystra on his second missionary journey we read that the brothers at Lystra and Iconium spoke well of Timothy (Acts 16:1-2). Paul was so impressed with him that he wanted to take him along on the journey. However, Timothy was of Jewish descent through his mother but had not been circumcised. This would have prevented him speaking in the synagogues so Paul circumcised him (Acts 16:3).

From then on it seems Timothy was either a constant companion of Paul, or was away on errands that Paul sent him on. First they travelled throughout Phrygia and Galatia, and eventually arrived at the coastal town of Troas. From there it was a boat trip up to Neapolis and then overland to Philippi. After that it was down to Thessalonica where there was strong opposition so they moved on to Berea, where they were well received. However, Jews from Thessalonica came and stirred up trouble. Paul was hurriedly sent to the coast to catch a boat bound for Athens, but Timothy and Silas stayed at Berea (Acts 17:14).

Timothy then joined Paul in Athens to let him know what was going on in Thessalonica and Berea and having heard the news, Paul sent him back to Thessalonica (1 Thessalonians 3:1-6).

---

[1] For more on the person of Timothy and his activities see Michael Penny's *Timothy: The Man* published by The Open Bible Trust

Paul moved on to Corinth where, some time later, Silas and Timothy joined him (Acts 18:5) and they were there when Paul wrote his first letter to the Thessalonians (1 Thessalonians 1:1; 3:6). They were still in Corinth with Paul when he wrote the second letter (2 Thessalonians 1:1) but Paul may have left them in Corinth (Acts 18:18). Timothy was with Paul in Ephesus on his third missionary journey, and this may have been when Paul sent him to Corinth to deal with a difficult situation (1 Corinthians 4:17; 16:10). Timothy may have been with Paul when he wrote 1 Corinthians, but he was definitely with him when Paul wrote 2 Corinthians (2 Corinthians 1:1). And sometime, Timothy had preached in Corinth (2 Corinthians 1:19).

Eventually Paul sent him and Erastus ahead to Macedonia (Acts 19:22) and joined him there later and they travelled through that area, and went down to Greece where they spent three months (Acts 20:1-4). From there he wrote to the Romans, and Timothy was with him (Romans 16:21), and then travelled with Paul back to Macedonia and went on ahead to Troas (Acts 20:4-5).

He may well have travelled with Paul onto Jerusalem and been around during Paul's imprisonment in Caesarea. However, he was definitely with Paul in Rome during his two year imprisonment (Acts 28:30). Early on in that imprisonment Paul wrote Colossians, and Timothy was with him (Colossians 1:1), and towards the end of that time he wrote Philippians, and Timothy was still with him (Philippians 1:1).

From all this activity we can see that Timothy was dynamic; going here, doing this, preaching, staying behind to sort out problems and calm the situation, going on ahead to pacify and prepare the ground. And perhaps the greatest testimony to Timothy is found in Philippians 2:19-23. There we read:

I hope in the Lord Jesus to send Timothy to you soon, that I also may be cheered when I receive news about you. I have no one else like him, who takes a genuine interest in your welfare. For everyone looks out for his own interests, not those of Jesus Christ. But you know that Timothy has proved himself, because as a son with his father he has served with me in the work of the gospel. I hope, therefore, to send him as soon as I see how things go with me.

However, within two or three years of writing Philippians, Paul wrote 1 Timothy and then, a little later, 2 Timothy. In these letters we get the impression that Timothy has altered. He is encouraged by Paul to fan into flame the gift of teaching which had been given to him, (1 Timothy 4:14; 2 Timothy 1:6-7). He seems to have lost his dynamism, and was showing signs of timidity. Why was that? Let us look at the letter and see if we can gain some insight into this man and learn from what Paul wrote to him.

1 Timothy
Chapter 1

1 Timothy
Chapter 1

1 Timothy 1:1-2: Paul, an apostle of Christ Jesus by the command of God our Saviour and of Christ Jesus our hope, To Timothy my true son in the faith: Grace, mercy and peace from God the Father and Christ Jesus our Lord.

Paul was an apostle of Christ Jesus by the command of God and, in all his letters except 2 Thessalonians and Philemon; he introduced himself as an 'apostle', literally 'one that is sent'. And here he reminded Timothy that he had been sent, commissioned, by none other than Christ Jesus. A modern day ambassador, in a foreign country, can say only what the government of his home country instructs him to say. He must represent the 'party line', as he is his home government's representative in that foreign country. Similarly, as an apostle of Christ Jesus, Paul could preach and teach only what Christ had given him, as he was Christ's representative in this foreign world, for Christians are citizens of heaven (Philippians 3:20).

He was an apostle by the command of God and of Jesus Christ our 'hope'. Today, when most people use the word 'hope', there is always an element of uncertainty. People 'hope' they will win a raffle. When invited to a function some may say that they 'hope' to come, but they are not 'confident' that they will be able to. However, the 'hope' that we have in Christ is a 'confident expectation' (*elpis*).

Paul called Timothy his 'true son' in the faith. It seems, then, that Timothy, who lived in Lystra, was saved under Paul's ministry when the apostle was on his first missionary journey. Sometime later when, on his second missionary journey, Paul returned to Lystra and found that Timothy was well spoken of by the Christians in both Lystra and Iconium.

A common opening in all of Paul's letters is to combine the words 'grace' and 'peace', but in both letters to Timothy he added 'mercy' – I wonder why!

'Grace' (Greek, *charis*) was a common Greek greeting, and the idea was one of joy and pleasure, of brightness and beauty, and *charis* gives us the English word 'charm'. When used by the Greeks to each other it probably did not have any great depth, similar, perhaps, to the American 'Have a nice day!' However, Paul takes this word, links it with *eirene / shalom*, and associates it with "God the Father of our Lord Jesus Christ". This is no *ordinary* grace; this is the grace of God and everything for man's greatest good comes from Him.

'Peace' (Greek, *eirene*) was the normal Jewish greeting and equivalent to the Hebrew *shalom*. However, our understanding of 'peace' is deficient. For us it often means the absence of war, freedom from terrorism, the absence of evil. When the Jews greeted each other with *"Shalom!"*, it was a positive peace, desiring the total well-being of the person addressed, wanting for them the highest good that comes from God. As Psalm 85:10 puts it:

> Love and faithfulness meet together,
> Righteousness and peace kiss each other.

'Mercy' is the word *eleos* and means 'tender mercy', 'compassion'. All three – grace, mercy and peace – are from God the Father and the Lord Jesus Christ, but why has Paul added this 'tender mercy', this 'compassion' of God? We mentioned in the introduction that Timothy, who was with Paul on much of his second and third missionary journeys, and who was with Paul in Rome, was a tower of strength during those arduous years. However, from both of the letters that Paul wrote to him it seems as if Timothy was no longer so strong, neither physically (1 Timothy 5:23) nor spiritually (1 Timothy 4:14; 2 Timothy 1:6). Maybe his lack of spirituality was due to his poor health and Paul deals with this situation gently, encouraging Timothy to use again his gift and reminding him that God is a compassionate and understanding God, full of tender mercy.

1 Timothy 1:3-4: As I urged you when I went into Macedonia, stay there in Ephesus so that you may command certain men not to teach false doctrines any longer nor to devote themselves to myths and endless genealogies.

On his third missionary journey Paul stayed in Ephesus and sent Timothy to Macedonia (Acts 19:22). Here we have the opposite situation with Timothy remaining in Ephesus and Paul going on to Macedonia. This, amongst other things in the Pastorals (e.g. Paul's visit to Crete, Titus 1:5, a place he never visited in Acts with Titus) indicates that after his two year imprisonment in Rome (Acts 28:30) Paul was released and undertook a fourth missionary journey.

Timothy was left in Ephesus to command certain men not to teach and devote themselves to such things as false doctrines, myths and genealogies. As Timothy would have no jurisdiction or authority outside of the church, these were Christian men within the church. What were they teaching?

The specifics are not spelt out here but we do know from other parts of Scripture that some of the false doctrines which had crept into various churches were:

> Gentiles had to be circumcised to be saved (Acts 15:1);
> Gentiles had to obey the Law of Moses (Acts 15:5);
> There was no resurrection of the dead (1 Corinthians 15:12);
> Some worshipped angels (Colossians 2:18);
> Christ, as God, did not have a real, human body (1 John 4:2-3; 2 John 7).

The first two of these seemed to have been propagated by Jewish Christians, while the last three were more of a problem for Gentiles who had embraced the faith.

'False doctrines' is the Greek *heterodidaskaleo*, from *hetero* (other) and *didaskaleo* (teaching). J N D Kelly[2] translates this 'teach novelties' and William Barclay[3] has 'teach erroneous novelties'. However, there does not seem to be anything implicit in the Greek to indicate these were solely 'new' teaching, but if there is, then this would refer to early Gnosticism and its teaching that everything physical was evil and so Christ did not have a human body.

---

[2] *The Pastoral Epistles;* page 41
[3] *The Daily Study Bible; The Letters to Timothy, Titus & Philemon*; page 25

'Myths' is the word *muthoi* and means 'tales' or a 'fables'. What 'tales' or 'fables' were these people teaching? The world where Timothy found himself was full of Greek mythology, and the people and their poets liked to hear and write "romantic and fictitious tales… how some god came down to earth and founded the city or took in marriage some mortal maid and founded a family.[4]" Paul refers also to 'godless' myths in 2 Timothy 4:4 and 'Jewish' myths in Titus 1:14.

And why the 'endless genealogies'? 'Endless' should not be taken literally. The Greek is *aperantos* and can mean 'interminable' or 'unrestrained'. This, again, may have been a problem with Jewish Christians who liked to trace their genealogy back to Abraham, and may have gone on about it 'interminably'. At one time, such a genealogy may have been important, but not any longer (Colossians 3:11). However, the Greeks were not free of this either. Alexander the Great had a mythological genealogy that traced him back to such people as Achilles and Hercules. That was certainly an 'unrestrained' genealogy!

Circumcision and the Law, with its commandments and ordinances, were done away with at the end of Acts when, following the last pronouncement of Isaiah's prophecy of judgment upon the nation of Israel, God's salvation was sent directly to the Gentiles, independently of Israel (Acts 28:25-28). Paul wrote about this in Ephesians 2:14-16 and Colossians 2:11,14-16. The important issue from then on was not obedience to the Mosaic Law but faith in Christ; those were "a shadow of the things which were to come; the reality, however, is found in Christ" (Colossians 2:17). As a result "there is no Greek or Jew,

---

[4] *The Daily Study Bible; The Letters to Timothy, Titus & Philemon*; page 26

circumcised or uncircumcised" (Colossians 3:11). Thus genealogies back to Abraham, circumcision on the eighth day, and following the rituals of the Mosaic Law meant nothing compared to "the surpassing greatness of knowing Christ Jesus my Lord" (Philippians 3:7-9).

1 Timothy 1:5-6: These promote controversies rather than God's work - which is by faith. The goal of this command is love, which comes from a pure heart and a good conscience and a sincere faith. Some have wandered away from these and turned to meaningless talk.

Such false doctrine, myths and genealogies served only to foster controversies amongst Christians, and especially between the Jewish and Gentile Christians of that day. As such the believers spent their time bickering and arguing, and not getting on with God's work, especially the work of preaching a gospel of salvation by grace through faith in Jesus Christ.

Paul's strong words were driven by a love which comes from a pure heart, a good conscience and a sincere faith. He is concerned about people he dearly cared for. Some had wandered away from the basics of the faith and were now involved with meaningless talk.

1 Timothy 1:7-11: They want to be teachers of the law, but they do not know what they are talking about or what they so confidently affirm. We know that the law is good if one uses it properly. We also know that law is made not for the righteous but for lawbreakers and rebels, the ungodly and sinful, the unholy and irreligious; for those who kill their fathers or mothers, for murderers, for adulterers and perverts, for slave traders and liars and perjurers - and for whatever else is

contrary to the sound doctrine that conforms to the glorious gospel of the blessed God, which he entrusted to me.

It would seem that some of the Christians were more concerned with teaching the Law of Moses, and this was most likely Jewish Christians. During the time covered by the Acts of the Apostles this might have been appropriate, but not any longer. It was right and proper to teach the Mosaic Law to Jews not only throughout Old Testament times but also during the time when Christ was on earth, and during the period covered by the Acts of the Apostles. However at the end of Acts, as we have seen, that Law, with its commandments and ordinances, was abolished. However, it was never appropriate to teach that Mosaic Law to Gentiles. The Jerusalem Council of Acts 15 had issued a letter stating that the Gentiles did not need to be circumcised, nor keep the Law of Moses. Hence, those Jewish Christians who continued teaching the whole of the Law of Moses did not know what they were on about.

There were parts of the Law, however, that were good, if it was used properly. In 2 Timothy 3:16-17 we read:

> All Scripture is God-breathed and is useful for teaching, rebuking, correcting and training in righteousness, so that the man of God may be thoroughly equipped for every good work.

Thus even the Law of Moses, if used properly, was beneficial and Paul indicated that it was the moral, practical teaching which was applicable to both the Jewish and Gentile Christians of his day, and today. The Law made clear that such things as murder, adultery and sexual perversion, slave trading, lying and perjury were all wrong, as were many other things which went against the sound doctrine of the Christian of faith. The ceremonial and dietary parts of the Mosaic Law, however, were no longer applicable, but the moral teaching was, and still is today.

1 Timothy 1:12-17: I thank Christ Jesus our Lord, who has given me strength, that he considered me faithful, appointing me to his service. Even though I was once a blasphemer and a persecutor and a violent man, I was shown mercy because I acted in ignorance and unbelief. The grace of our Lord was poured out on me abundantly, along with the faith and love that are in Christ Jesus. Here is a trustworthy saying that deserves full acceptance: Christ Jesus came into the world to save sinners - of whom I am the worst. But for that very reason I was shown mercy so that in me, the worst of sinners, Christ Jesus might display his unlimited patience as an example for those who would believe on him and receive eternal life. Now to the King eternal, immortal, invisible, the only God, be honour and glory for ever and ever. Amen.

Although saved on the Damascus Road and told that he was to be sent to the Gentiles and their kings and to the people of Israel (Acts 9:15-17), it was not until fourteen years later that he was appointed and sent off in service (Galatians 2:1-10; Acts 13:1-3). Some of those years he spent in Arabia (Galatians 1:17) but much of the time he was in Tarsus, in the region of Syria and Cilicia (Galatians 1:21; Acts 9:30). We may not know precisely what Paul did for all those years, but whatever it was, he was considered faithful.

However, before his conversion he persecuted the church. We read that he was there at the stoning of Stephen (Acts 7:57-58), after which great persecution broke out against the church, and then Saul (Paul) tried to destroy the church, dragging off

Christian men and women to prison (Acts 8:1-3). For a long period of time he issued murderous threats against the disciples and his excursion into Damascus to arrest Christians was not the first foreign city he visited for this purpose (Acts 26:11; note, foreign cities, plural). Paul did all this because he did not believe that Jesus was the Christ (Messiah), the son of God; he was ignorant of the correct teaching of the Hebrew Scriptures (our Old Testament).

Because he acted in unbelief and ignorance he was shown mercy, that tender, compassionate mercy he mentioned in verse 2. As a result the grace of God was poured out on him abundantly, resulting in Paul having great love and faith in Christ Jesus. And if Paul, who mentions twice that he was the 'worst' of sinners, could find forgiveness and grace and mercy, then so could anyone else. All his blasphemy, persecution and murder had been forgiven; he was loved and forgiven by God. No wonder Paul, possibly falling to his knees, utters "Now to the King eternal, immortal, invisible, the only God, be honour and glory for ever and ever. Amen."

1 Timothy 1:18-20: Timothy, my son, I give you this instruction in keeping with the prophecies once made about you, so that by following them you may fight the good fight, holding on to faith and a good conscience. Some have rejected these and so have shipwrecked their faith. Among them are Hymenaeus and Alexander, whom I have handed over to Satan to be taught not to blaspheme.

The instruction(s) Paul is about to give Timothy come a little later in the next chapter. They were in accordance with certain prophecies made about Timothy. This is mentioned again in 1 Timothy 4:14, where Timothy is told not to neglect a gift which was given him through a prophetic message when the elders laid their hands on him (see also 2 Timothy 1:6).

During the period covered by the Acts, the Apostles displayed all types of miraculous gifts, but each individual believer possessed one (1 Corinthians 12:7-11;27-31). Although the majority of these ceased at the end of Acts, a few continued for a little while. Timothy's gift may have been that of teaching, a gift which did continue (Ephesians 4:11), and Timothy is told to teach by Paul (1 Timothy 4:11,13; 6:2). If this was the case, Timothy's charge was to teach others the instructions Paul was about to give him. These instructions were for the benefit of others. If Timothy used his gift and followed the prophecies made about him, he would be fighting the good fight, holding on to the faith and would have a good conscience. It was essential that he teach these instructions to others, for some who had failed to follow them had shipwrecked their faith, and Paul names two such people.

But what did Paul mean when he wrote that he had handed them over to Satan to be taught not to blaspheme? The expression also comes in 1 Corinthians 5:5. A man had had an incestuous sexual relationship and the Corinthian church had done nothing about the situation. They were told:

> Hand this man over to Satan, so that the sinful nature may be destroyed and his spirit saved on the day of the Lord. (1 Corinthians 5:5)

In both of these passages (1 Corinthians 5:5 and 1 Timothy 1:20) this is done, hoping for a positive outcome; that the man's spirit may be saved, and that Hymaneaus and Alexander would learn not to blaspheme.

One possibility is that they should be put out of the church, and left to the world, which is Satan's domain (Ephesians 2:1-2). However, this, on its own, would not bring about a change in the people. To this may be added the idea of suffering, or some form of judgment. Elymas the sorcerer was struck blind for opposing Paul (Acts 13:8-11). Some of the Corinthian Christians were struck with sickness and death for gluttony and drunkenness at the Lord's Supper (1 Corinthians 11:29-30). James wrote of sickness caused by sin (James 5:14-16). Thus just as Job learnt from the suffering he underwent, a suffering inflicted by Satan, so Paul wanted these men to learn, but did it work? In some cases it seems to have; see 2 Corinthians 7:8-13.

In his second letter to Timothy we read of them again. Hymenaeus is mentioned in 2 Timothy 2:17, teaching the error that the resurrection of believers is past. And in 2 Timothy 4:14 Paul wrote that Alexander had done him great harm, although we are not given the details of what he did.

1 Timothy
Chapter 2

1 Timothy
Chapter 2

1 Timothy 2:1-4: I urge, then, first of all, that requests, prayers, intercession and thanksgiving be made for everyone - for kings and all those in authority, that we may live peaceful and quiet lives in all godliness and holiness. This is good, and pleases God our Saviour, who wants all men to be saved[5] and to come to a knowledge of the truth.

The first instruction is not unlike that given at the end of Ephesians, when Paul wrote "pray in the Spirit on all occasions with all kinds of prayers and requests. With this in mind, be alert and always keep on praying for all the saints" (Ephesians 6:18). There the prayers were for "all the saints". Here it is wider; it is for "everyone" and especially for kings and those in authority – and that would have included Caesar Nero. The focus of the prayers is for a peaceful and quiet society, one in which Christians are not persecuted and one where Christians can live lives full of godliness and holiness. Such a society and such lives enable Christians to share the gospel of salvation with others, and teach them about the love and grace and mercy of God. This pleases God who wants all men to be saved and come to a knowledge of the truth. However, such preaching and teaching is difficult in a society which opposes and persecutes Christians or in a society full of lawlessness, disorder and violence.

---

[5] Appendix 2 deals with the statement that God wants all men to be saved.

But why did Paul want prayers for such people as Nero? Perhaps Paul could see a change for the worse coming. Throughout Paul's life he had benefitted from the *pax Romana*[6]; the Roman peace. There was peace and prosperity throughout the eastern half of the Roman Empire. It allowed freedom and safe travel throughout the Mediterranean world. The Apostle Paul could travel from country to country with greater freedom, and possibly greater safety, than we can today. He needed no passport and no visas. He could just "go", travelling along superbly engineered roads, sailing seas policed by Roman galleons. Everywhere he went he could expect the protection of Roman law, but could he sense the change that was soon to come, the persecution of Christians by Caesar Nero?

1 Timothy 2:5-7: For there is one God and one mediator between God and men, the man Christ Jesus, who gave himself as a ransom for all men - the testimony given in its proper time. And for this purpose I was appointed a herald and an apostle - I am telling the truth, I am not lying - and a teacher of the true faith to the Gentiles.

God wants all men to be saved and come to a knowledge of the truth, especially the truth that there is only one God and only one mediator, Jesus Christ. In Paul's day there were other gods and other ideas about how people could get to the next life, and the one true God had to vie with them, as did the one Saviour and mediator.

Today we have 'other' faiths and 'other' religions and 'other' ideas about what is the next life and how people can get there. Our job remains the same of preaching salvation by grace through

---

[6] For more on the *pax Romana* visit www.obt.org.uk and click on 'free downloads' and then on 'The Unexpected'.

faith in Jesus Christ, who gave himself a ransom for all[7], and teaching people about the one true God, His love, grace and mercy. That was the purpose for which Paul was appointed a herald and an apostle. He alone is the one the Scriptures call "the Apostle to the Gentiles" (Romans 11:13). His task was to teach the 'true' faith to the Gentiles; that was also Timothy's task, and today it is ours.

1 Timothy 2:8-10: I want men everywhere to lift up holy hands in prayer, without anger or disputing. I also want women to dress modestly, with decency and propriety, not with braided hair or gold or pearls or expensive clothes, but with good deeds, appropriate for women who profess to worship God.

This must not be misread as Paul saying only men should pray in church. From what he wrote in 1 Corinthians 11:4-5 both men and women prayed in the Corinthian church and Paul had no objections to that. Here Paul wrote that when men prayed they should not do so if they were angry or had been disputing; they should pray with holy hands. We need to remember that such things as disputes and anger can grieve the Holy Spirit of God with whom we are sealed (Ephesians 4:30-31).

And women, when they prayed in church, should dress appropriately. In 1 Corinthians he said that their head should be covered, and here he states that they should dress modestly, with decency and propriety and not with braided hair. In 1 Corinthians, and here, the Christian women should take care not to appear brazen, flaunting their femininity. In Corinth the temple of Zeus

---

[7] For more on Christ being 'A ransom for all men' see Appendix 2

had 1,000 priestesses (prostitutes) and in Ephesus, where Timothy was, prostitution was also rife. Christian women should distance themselves from such females.

But not only that, those women who were wealthy should not flaunt their wealth by appearing in church wearing gold and pearls and their most expensive clothes. Rather they should clothe themselves with good deeds. Peter gives similar advice to Christian women whose husbands had not yet come to believe in Jesus.

> Wives, in the same way be submissive to your husbands so that, if any of them do not believe the word, they may be won over without words by the behaviour of their wives, when they see the purity and reverence of your lives. Your beauty should not come from outward adornment, such as braided hair and the wearing of gold jewellery and fine clothes. Instead, it should be that of your inner self, the unfading beauty of a gentle and quiet spirit, which is of great worth in God's sight. (1 Peter 3:1-4)

1 Timothy 2:11-12: A woman should learn in quietness and full submission. I do not permit a woman to teach or to have authority over a man; she must be silent.

The word translated 'woman' is *gune* which in many places is translated 'wife', and the word translated 'man' is *aner* which in other places is translated 'husband'. Thus this passage could be rendered:

A wife should learn in quietness and full submission. I do not permit a wife to teach or to have authority over her husband; she must be silent.

If this is the case, what Paul states is very similar to what Peter wrote in 1 Peter 3:1-4, quoted above, and it is in harmony with 1 Corinthians 14:33-35 which states:

> As in all the congregations of the saints, women should remain silent in the churches. They are not allowed to speak, but must be in submission, as the Law says. If they want to inquire about something, they should ask their own husbands at home; for it is disgraceful for a woman to speak in the church.

Here women are told to learn from their own husbands. However, the passage should not be misunderstood. It is referring to women talking to each other and discussing during the service, and so causing disruption. It is *not* saying that women could not take part in the service. Earlier in 1 Corinthians, Paul had referred to both men and women praying and prophesying in the service (1 Corinthians 11:5).

For a more detailed treatment of 1 Timothy 2:11-12, and the role of women in the church, see Appendix 1 and also pages 234-240 of *Woman to Woman* edited by Sylvia Penny and published by The Open Bible Trust.

1 Timothy 2:13-14: For Adam was formed first, then Eve. And Adam was not the one deceived; it was the woman who was deceived and became a sinner.

How we understand these verses depends upon whether we view the preceding verses as dealing with women / men relationships or the wife / husband relationship. If the former, then some conclude that women should not teach men as women are more easily deceived and could then lead men astray with wrong teaching, but the majority who hold this view are perfectly happy for women to teach children. However, if it be true that women are more easily deceived then they are far more likely to lead ill-informed children astray than they are mature men who would know far more about the Bible and its teaching than the youngsters.

If limited to the wife / husband situation it makes more sense. Eve was, indeed, deceived and, because of his closeness to her, Adam was swayed by his wife when she offered him the fruit. It is true that our wives have a bigger effect on our thinking and lives than any other person; often that is for the good, but it may not always be. (For a more detailed discussion on these verses see Appendix 1.)

1 Timothy 2:15: But women will be saved through childbearing - if they continue in faith, love and holiness with propriety.

Here, Paul cannot be referring to be 'saved' for eternal life. That salvation is by grace through faith in Christ, not by works, not even the wonderful work of childbearing. The word for 'saved' is the Greek *sozo* which takes a variety of meanings, and is translated by such expressions as, heal, preserve, save (self), do well, be (make) whole.

In 1 Timothy 4:16 Paul uses this expression again. There we read, "Watch your life and doctrine closely. Persevere in them, because if you do, you will save both yourself and your hearers."

Again, this cannot refer to initial salvation for eternal life. Hebrews 7:25 talks of being saved to the 'uttermost' (*KJV*) or saved 'completely' (*NIV*) and this may be referring to believers going on to maturity (Hebrews 6:1). All are exhorted to work out their salvation (Philippians 2:12) and part of the working out of salvation for the women of Paul's day was to have children and raise them, setting them an example by living a life which exhibited faith, love and holiness with propriety.

It would seem, then, that Paul's line of argument in this passage is that women should not teach their husbands and that their main task is raising their family. The word for 'childbearing' means more than just giving birth, and involves child rearing. (For a more detailed treatment of the different interpretations of this verse see pages 212-216 of *Woman to Woman* edited by Sylvia Penny and published by The Open Bible Trust.)

1 Timothy
Chapter 3

1 Timothy
Chapter 3

1 Timothy 3:1: Here is a trustworthy saying: If anyone sets his heart on being an overseer, he desires a noble task.

Earlier the church was run by Apostles, gifts of the ascended Christ, given until the diverse church of Jewish and Gentile Christians, which came out of the Acts period, came to a unity (Ephesians 4:11-13). These were being replaced by 'overseers' (*NIV*), 'bishops' (*KJV*) – see also Philippians 1:1 and Titus 1:7. The Apostles were Christ appointed, but these overseers were to be appointed by human beings.

Today some churches make much of the idea that a man should feel he has had a 'call' from God, and then others have to decide whether or not this 'call' is genuine; a situation which can lead to much disharmony and heartache if they decide not to accept the person. However, 'call' is not mentioned here. It is quite simply and honestly stated that a person may 'set his heart' on being an overseer, and if he does, he should not be considered as being 'pushy' and having too high an opinion of himself. Such a person desires a noble task, but is he suitable? That is the issue. In the following verses Paul laid out a blueprint of the character of a person who would be suitable for such a leadership position.

1 Timothy 3: 2-7: Now the overseer must be above reproach, the husband of but one wife, temperate, self-controlled, respectable, hospitable, able to teach, not given to

drunkenness, not violent but gentle, not quarrelsome, not a lover of money.

> **He must manage his own family well and see that his children obey him with proper respect. (If anyone does not know how to manage his own family, how can he take care of God's church?)**

> **He must not be a recent convert, or he may become conceited and fall under the same judgment as the devil.**

> **He must also have a good reputation with outsiders, so that he will not fall into disgrace and into the devil's trap.**

This is all very sane and sensible. He must be of impeccable character, not only within the church, but also with those outside the church.

He must be a good family man, with obedient and respectful children, and having but one wife. In those days some areas allowed polygamy, but God's ideal was one man and one wife for life (Matthew 19:4-8). If a man who had more than one wife became a Christian, he could not leave the other wives destitute; he should continue to love and support them, but he could not be an overseer.

And he must not be a recent convert, no matter how keen, enthusiastic and talented that new believer may be. Such a person must be cared for and protected, as conceit and pride may creep in, which is what happened to Satan (Ezekiel 28:15,17).

An overseer must also be able to teach, which means he must have a good knowledge of what the Scriptures teach about sin and salvation, death and eternal life, right and wrong, Christ's death and resurrection, and about much more beside.

1 Timothy 3:8-13: Deacons, likewise, are to be men worthy of respect, sincere, not indulging in much wine, and not pursuing dishonest gain. They must keep hold of the deep truths of the faith with a clear conscience. They must first be tested; and then if there is nothing against them, let them serve as deacons.

> **In the same way, their wives are to be women worthy of respect, not malicious talkers but temperate and trustworthy in everything. A deacon must be the husband of but one wife and must manage his children and his household well.**

> **Those who have served well gain an excellent standing and great assurance in their faith in Christ Jesus.**

'Overseers' must be able to teach and it would seem that they were responsible for what was taught in the church, the doctrine, the meetings etc. The duties of 'deacons', on the other hand, covered issues not related to teaching. The first time we come across such a distinction is in Acts 6:1-6 when a problem arose with the distribution of food within the church. The Apostles stated that it would not be right for them to neglect the ministry of the word and "wait on tables". Seven men were appointed and given this responsibility. They were not called 'deacons' in this passage and the word for 'deacon' is *diakonos*, probably from *diako* (to run on errands) and means an attendant; i.e. (with the genitive case) a waiter (at table or in other menial duties); see Strong's *Exhaustive Concordance and Lexicon.*

If the duties of deacons are considered more menial or more practical than those of overseers, they, none-the-less, were still required to be of the highest character. In fact there is little difference between the two lists of requirements. There is no stipulation that a deacon should be able to teach, but he needs to know the deep truths of the faith and keep hold of them. Again, he should not be a recent convert, as implied by the statement, he should "first be tested".

Also, conditions are laid down for a deacon's wife[8], but one suspects these would also be expected of an overseer's wife.

1 Timothy 3:14-15: Although I hope to come to you soon, I am writing you these instructions so that, if I am delayed, you will know how people ought to conduct themselves in God's household, which is the church of the living God, the pillar and foundation of the truth.

As mentioned earlier, after his two years in prison (Acts 28:30) Paul was released and undertook another missionary journey. From 1 Timothy 1:3 we see he had visited Ephesus and left Timothy there while he went to Macedonia. He wrote to Timothy telling him he anticipated returning soon, but if he did not make it back, the instructions in this letter showed how people were to

---

[8] The *NIV* has a footnote on 'wives' suggesting it could be translated 'deaconesses'. Although Phoebe is called a servant (Romans 16:1; *NIV & KJV*) the Greek is *diakonos* and she may well have been a deaconess. Here, however, the Greek is *gune*, meaning wife or woman.

conduct themselves in God's household. God's household is the church, a term he uses only here and in Ephesians 2:19. This church is the pillar and foundation of the truth, or at least it should be. In some churches today the very authority of the Bible is questioned and its teachings are undermined.

1 Timothy 3:16: Beyond all question, the mystery of godliness is great:

> **He appeared in a body,**
> **was vindicated by the Spirit,**
> **was seen by angels,**
> **was preached among the nations,**
> **was believed on in the world,**
> **was taken up in glory.**

One of the truths that the church is to uphold is the great mystery of godliness, which deals with the incarnation: He (God) appeared in a body. In the person of Christ, God became man; He was "manifest in the flesh" (*KJV*).

If these events are meant to be sequential then Paul may have had in mind something like the following. The Spirit came down on Him at His baptism; angels strengthened Him at the end of His temptations in the wilderness (Matthew 4:11). When on earth He was preached among all the people of Israel, even to those Jews of the dispersion who returned to Jerusalem on feast days, and some of those believed on Him and went back to their home countries (Acts 18:24-26; 19:1-3). After his resurrection He ascended into heaven and now sits at God's right hand dwelling in glory (Colossians 3:4).

However, when writing Paul may not have meant the events to have been taken either sequentially or exhaustively. In that case we could add an angel told Joseph to take the Baby to Egypt and told him when to take the Child back, and angels strengthened Christ in the Garden of Gethsemane (Luke 22:43). And after His resurrection people like Paul preached Him throughout the Roman Empire and beyond, and many people believed.

This short, but great, hymn contains some of the doctrines which should be taught by the church to make it the pillar and foundation of truth.

1 Timothy
Chapter 4

1 Timothy
Chapter 4

1 Timothy 4:1-2: The Spirit clearly says that in later times some will abandon the faith and follow deceiving spirits and things taught by demons. Such teachings come through hypocritical liars, whose consciences have been seared as with a hot iron.

Some people, whenever they see expressions like 'the last days' or 'latter days' or 'later times', think these expressions always refer to the days just preceding Christ's second coming. However, in a number of places where the *KJV* has "in the last days" or "in the latter days", the *NIV* has "in days to come" (e.g. Genesis 49:1; Numbers 24:14; see also *NASV* which has the same as the *NIV*). Thus Paul may be warning Timothy of what is to face him later in his life, rather than informing him of what is to happen in the distant future.[9]

How did the deceiving spirits operate? And what sorts of things were taught by demons? First note that Paul says nothing about demon 'possession', a subject I have written about in detail elsewhere; see *The Miracles of the* Apostles Published by The Open Bible Trust. Demon possession took place when our Lord was on earth and just afterwards, during the time covered by the Acts of the Apostles, and no believer in Christ was, or could be, possessed by a demon. And that is true today because when we believe the gospel of salvation we are sealed with the Holy Spirit

---

[9] For a full treatment of this see *The Last Days! When?* By Michael Penny, published by The Open Bible Trust.

who possesses us until the day of redemption (Ephesians 1:13-14; 4:30). However, believers could 'follow' deceiving spirits and 'follow' things taught by demons.

It would seem that such teaching came through hypocrites who lie, and who have no conscience about what they are doing. One such example may be what Paul wrote about earlier:

> Do not let anyone who delights in false humility and the worship of angels disqualify you for the prize. Such a person goes into great detail about what he has seen, and his unspiritual mind puffs him up with idle notions. (Colossians 2:18)

This, of course, was much more likely to be a problem experienced by Gentile Christians as no Jew would worship anyone other than God (Exodus 20:2-3).

John also wrote about people who deceived others by what they taught.

> Many deceivers, who do not acknowledge Jesus Christ as coming in the flesh, have gone out into the world. Any such person is the deceiver and the antichrist. (2 John 7)

> This is how you can recognize the Spirit of God: Every spirit that acknowledges that Jesus Christ has come in the flesh is from God, but every spirit that does not acknowledge Jesus is not from God. This is the spirit of the antichrist, which you have heard is coming and even now is already in the world. (1 John 4:2-3)

What else was taught by these people?

1 Timothy 4:3-5: They forbid people to marry and order them to abstain from certain foods, which God created to be received with thanksgiving by those who believe and who know the truth. For everything God created is good, and nothing is to be rejected if it is received with thanksgiving, because it is consecrated by the word of God and prayer.

The forbidding of marriage and the abstention of food was a part of Gnosticism which started in those times and built up over the next hundred years or more. Some gnostics taught that everything material was evil and, as food was material, it was evil and, as far as possible, it should not be eaten. Similarly the body was material and so evil. Thus people should abstain from marriage and procreation.

Irenaeus wrote at the end of the second century criticising the followers of Saturinus, whom some see as the founder of Syrian Gnosticism. They declared "that marriage and generation are from Satan. Many likewise abstain from animal food, and draw away multitudes by a feigned temperance of this kind" (*Against Heresies*, 1,24,2).

Some have suggested that the abstention from certain foods would come from those Christian Jews who thought they should continue observing the Mosaic Law, even though it had been abolished by God at the end of the Acts Period (Colossians 2:13-16; Ephesians 2:14-16). In doing this they were clearly wrong and did not understand the new freedom they now had in Christ (Colossians 2:17). However, one could hardly accuse them of following deceiving spirits and things taught by demons.

However, the gnostic teaching to abstain from meat went against the express command of God (Genesis 9:3). And the command to abstain from marriage ... we have seen the sad effects of this upon the celibate priesthood of the Catholic Church.

1 Timothy 4:6-8: If you point these things out to the brothers, you will be a good minister of Christ Jesus, brought up in the truths of the faith and of the good teaching that you have followed. Have nothing to do with godless myths and old wives' tales; rather, train yourself to be godly. For physical training is of some value, but godliness has value for all things, holding promise for both the present life and the life to come.

So Timothy was instructed to point out to people that there were deceiving spirits around and doctrines of demons, and that two of these dealt with forbidding to marry and forbidding certain foods. He needed to point this out to be a good minister of Christ and to balance these false teachings with good teaching and the truths of the faith. Also, to be a good minister, he was to have nothing to do with these, which are described as godless myths and old wives tales. Instead he was to focus on training to be godly.

Godless is *bebelos*, translated 'profane' in *KJV* and *ASV* as "profane and old wives tales". Timothy was in Ephesus and these profane old wives tales could be to do with Greek mythology and paganism. The goddess Artemis was worshipped there (Acts 19:24) and in Lystra they thought Barnabas was Zeus and Paul Hermes (Acts 14:11-13). The behaviour of some of the Greek gods was profane, and people enjoyed hearing of their escapades. Christians should have nothing to do with such stories (Ephesians 4:29).

Timothy was in Ephesus, the eastern half of the Roman Empire, the part greatly influenced by Greek culture, including the gymnasia with their athletics, fitness and physical prowess. Such physical fitness has, as we know, some good value, enabling us to live healthier and longer lives, but physical wellbeing by itself does not bring eternal life. However, godliness, living according to the teachings of Christ and the Bible, not only benefits us in this life (Christians in Britain live, on average, four years[10] longer than non-Christians), it also brings eternal value.

1 Timothy 4:9-11: This is a trustworthy saying[11] that deserves full acceptance (and for this we labour and strive), that we have put our hope in the living God, who is the Saviour of all men, and especially of those who believe. Command and teach these things.

A number of times Paul used the expression 'trustworthy saying' and he uses it to emphasise the importance of the teaching. Here he emphasises that we do not put our hope in physical fitness or dietary restrictions, but rather in the living God. And Timothy is told to both command and teach these things to the people in Ephesus.

Timothy was to teach people to put their hope in the living God who was not just the Saviour of the Jews, but of all men, Gentiles as well. Salvation was open to all, for God wishes[12] all men to be

---

[10] See the statistics from the UK Government Actuaries Department and Religious Trends quoted on page 2 of *Search* number 162 published by The Open Bible Trust.

[11] All the 'trustworthy sayings' are found in the Pastoral Epistles; see 1 Timothy 1:15; 3:1; 4:9; 2 Timothy 2:11; Titus 1:9; 3:8.

[12] 1 Timothy 2:4; George Ricker Berry, *The Interlinear Greek New Testament*.

saved. But are all saved? And do all have eternal life? See Appendix 2 for a discussion of these questions.

1 Timothy 4:12-14: Don't let anyone look down on you because you are young, but set an example for the believers in speech, in life, in love, in faith and in purity. Until I come, devote yourself to the public reading of Scripture, to preaching and to teaching. Do not neglect your gift, which was given you through a prophetic message when the body of elders laid their hands on you.

We do not know exactly how old Timothy was. He came on the scene in Acts 16:1, when Paul was on his second missionary journey. From then on he was with Paul, or carrying out tasks for the apostle. Since then more than ten or twelve years had gone by and Timothy was probably into his thirties, but compared to some of the Jewish scholars, and to some of the Greek philosophers, that would have been young. Thus he needed to live an exemplary life to avoid criticism and to set an example to other believers.

He also needed to be not just a private Christian, but a public one; preaching and teaching and reading the Scriptures in public places. When in Ephesus, on his third Missionary Journey, Paul had done this himself in the lecture hall of Tyrannus, so that all in the area had heard the word of the Lord (Acts 19:9). Timothy had the ability to do this, because a special gift, probably of teaching, had been given him by the Holy Spirit. However, it was possible to quench the Spirit (1 Thessalonians 5:19; *KJV*), and Timothy seems to have been in danger of doing this.

1 Timothy 4:15-16: Be diligent in these matters; give yourself wholly to them, so that everyone may see your progress. Watch your life and doctrine closely. Persevere in them,

because if you do, you will save both yourself and your hearers.

Timothy needed to be diligent and conscientious about reading the Scriptures and teaching and preaching in public places. But he also needed to watch what he did and what he taught very closely; there would be unsympathetic eyes on him, looking for places where they could criticise and condemn him. Therefore he needed to be an example to others, in speech, in life, in love and in purity. Also his doctrine needed to be good teaching based on the truths of the faith. He needed to persevere in these two – good living and good teaching – for in doing so he would save both himself and those who listened to him.

But what did Paul mean here by 'save'? Clearly Timothy, and everyone else, was saved by grace through faith in Christ, thus Paul could not have been referring to initial salvation. However, good living and good teaching would save him, and others, from untrue and unkind criticism from those who opposed them. And it is the same for Christians today. We open ourselves to criticism and opposition when either our life-style falls short of Christian standards, or we are unable to explain what we believe and why we believe it (1 Peter 3:15; Colossians 4:6). Thus we need to know what to do, and not do, and what to teach.

> 2 Timothy 3:14-17: But as for you, continue in what you have learned and have become convinced of, because you know those from whom you learned it, and how from infancy you have known the holy Scriptures, which are able to make you wise for salvation through faith in Christ Jesus. All Scripture is God-breathed and is useful for teaching, rebuking, correcting and training in

righteousness, so that the man of God may be thoroughly equipped for every good work.

This guidance, given by Paul to Timothy in his second letter, is also good advice for us. We need to know what the Scriptures teach about salvation, and what they say constitutes righteous living. In doing this we will be thoroughly equipped.

1 Timothy

Chapter 5

1 Timothy
Chapter 5

1 Timothy 5:1-2: Do not rebuke an older man harshly, but exhort him as if he were your father. Treat younger men as brothers, older women as mothers, and younger women as sisters, with absolute purity.

Here, in a couple of short sentences, Paul gives general instructions to Timothy on how to treat all people. However, a long section follows concerning the treatment of Christian widows. They needed to be looked after and in Jerusalem this had been a problem and had been dealt with by electing seven men to ensure that they were treated fairly (Acts 6:1). Widows, in the Law of Moses, were to be cared for by the community if they had no family to look after them, and neglect of them and their children was a serious sin (e.g. Isaiah 1:17). What was to happen in the Christian community which was not under the Law of Moses?

1 Timothy 5:3-4: Give proper recognition to those widows who are really in need. But if a widow has children or grandchildren, these should learn first of all to put their religion into practice by caring for their own family and so repaying their parents and grandparents, for this is pleasing to God.

The Mosaic Law made the people of Israel the first welfare state where the poor, the orphans, the fatherless and the widows were cared for. However, as with our benefit system, there were some who, for one reason or another, did not need the help but who, none-the-less, applied for it. Thus Paul wrote about the widows who were 'really' in need. Widows who had working children or grand-children should be supported by their families, and not by the church. Such behaviour was seen as putting their religion into practice and, again, had its origins in the Mosaic Law. And such a system, with children and grand-children supporting aged relatives, should be the system today to relieve pressure on the benefits system. However, that would not be popular amongst many, but it was not popular when our Lord was on earth. The Pharisees, in one of their many additions to the Law of Moses, had developed a scheme whereby people could be freed from supporting their parents.

> "For Moses said, 'Honour your father and your mother,' and, 'Anyone who curses his father or mother must be put to death.' But you say that if a man says to his father or mother: 'Whatever help you might otherwise have received from me is Corban' (that is, a gift devoted to God), then you no longer let him do anything for his father or mother. Thus you nullify the word of God by your tradition that you have handed down. And you do many things like that." (Mark 7:10-13)

1 Timothy 5:5-8: The widow who is really in need and left all alone puts her hope in God and continues night and day to pray and to ask God for help. But the widow who lives for pleasure is dead even while she lives. Give the people these instructions, too, so that no one may be open to blame. If anyone does not provide for his relatives, and especially for his immediate family, he has denied the faith and is worse than an unbeliever.

Here Paul contrasts two widows; those who are really in need (i.e. those who have no family), and those who 'live for pleasure'. It is not clear what Paul means by this second class. The Greek is *spatalo* and suggests "abandonment to pleasure and comfort[13]" but it does not imply sexual immorality or prostitution. Maybe these are the well-off widows who spent their money on themselves and pleasure, but were not using the wealth wisely, sharing and caring for others, an issue he deals with in chapter 6.

However, Paul returns to the theme of families caring for their own relatives, especially their immediate relatives. Not to do so was, indeed, a grave sin and would be seen as such by the non-Christian community. Thus those who ignored the needs of their relatives brought blame on the church and it would appear that the person has no real faith and so was no better, and in fact in some cases, was worse than an unbeliever, some of whom did look after their relatives.

1 Timothy 5:9-10: No widow may be put on the list of widows unless she is over sixty, has been faithful to her husband, and is well known for her good deeds, such as bringing up children, showing hospitality, washing the feet of the saints, helping those in trouble and devoting herself to all kinds of good deeds.

Paul begins to lay down some rules. Widows under sixty were likely to have living male relatives who should provide for them. However, as life expectancy was much lower in those days, if a woman did live into her sixties it may well be that any sons she may have had were dead. But being over sixty was not sufficient; she should be known to the community and known to have been not only a good wife, but one who did much good to the others.

---

[13] Page 114 *The Pastoral Epistles,* J N D Kelly

This would prevent other widows from the area joining the church not because they came to believe in Christ, but because they would be cared for – and we have a similar situation today where people from other countries come to Britain simply to claim benefits.

1 Timothy 5:11-15: As for younger widows, do not put them on such a list. For when their sensual desires overcome their dedication to Christ, they want to marry. Thus they bring judgment on themselves, because they have broken their first pledge. Besides, they get into the habit of being idle and going about from house to house. And not only do they become idlers, but also gossips and busybodies, saying things they ought not to. So I counsel younger widows to marry, to have children, to manage their homes and to give the enemy no opportunity for slander. Some have in fact already turned away to follow Satan.

The younger widows should not be put on the list. If they were supported by the church they would have time on their hands and could get into the habit of being idle, with nothing to do but going from home to home, visiting other women and gossiping, but there was also another danger with younger widows.

Their desire to be married may lead to them marrying non-Christian men. This desire could be so strong that it would overcome their dedication to Christ. In doing this they would break their first pledge, which was to Christ – not first in time, but first in priority. If they did that they would bring judgment on themselves and lose their reward in eternity (1 Corinthians 3:11-15). They could also end up following Satan. This was not 'Satan worship' but the non-Christian husband would be a worshipper of some idol or some pagan gods and, as was normal in those days, his wife would follow suit. Thus Paul counsels the younger widows to re-marry, i.e. marry a man who was a believer, and have children and manage her own home. That was the normal situation in those days and by doing that she would give those outside the church no opportunity to slander her.

1 Timothy 5:16: If any woman who is a believer has widows in her family, she should help them and not let the church be burdened with them, so that the church can help those widows who are really in need.

And the duty of providing relatives did not rest solely on the men; it was also the responsibility of the women in the family. Thus a widowed relative, whether that was her mother or grandmother, her sister or daughter, should be cared for.

1 Timothy 5:17-19: The elders who direct the affairs of the church well are worthy of double honour, especially those whose work is preaching and teaching. For the Scripture says, "Do not muzzle the ox while it is treading out the grain," and "The worker deserves his wages." Do not entertain an accusation against an elder unless it is brought by two or three witnesses.

Preparation for preaching and teaching takes much study, which takes time, thus robbing those who do so of the opportunity to work to earn money to support their families. As such they are worthy of payment, but Paul stated that they were worthy of 'double' honour, and the word translated honour (*time*) is elsewhere translated 'price'. Paul backs this up with two quotations, one from Deuteronomy 25:4, and one from Luke 10:7, the latter showing that by this time the Gospel of Luke was in circulation and known.

The elders who run the church are vulnerable. As we know today, many have a moan and a groan about their ministers. However, it can get more serious than that and Paul stated that lone accusation should be ignored; it needed at least two or three. This was not a special privilege for leaders. The principle of needing two or three witnesses to establish the truth of an accusation was enshrined in the Mosaic Law (e.g. Deuteronomy 17:6; 19:15; Matthew 18:16; 2 Corinthians 13:1; Hebrews 10:28), and this is an example of using the Law properly (1 Timothy 1:8).

1 Timothy 5:20-22: Those who sin are to be rebuked publicly, so that the others may take warning. I charge you, in the sight of God and Christ Jesus and the elect angels, to keep these instructions without partiality, and to do nothing out of favouritism. Do not be hasty in the laying on of hands, and do not share in the sins of others. Keep yourself pure.

'Rebuke' (v 1) and 'rebuke' (v 20) are two different Greek words. George Ricker Berry's *The Interlinear Greek New Testament* has "rebuke sharply" in verse 1 and "convict" in verse 20; the *ASV* has "reprove" (v 20). Christian leaders cannot turn a blind eye to sin, and neither can they let their flock continue in sin. There is always the need to admonish (Colossians 3:16), rebuke, reprove, convict. During the Acts period there had been the miracle of judgment where those who sinned were publically judged; e.g. Ananias and Sapphira (Acts 5:1-11); Herod Agrippa (Acts 12:19-23); Elymas (Acts 13:8-11).

Timothy was publically to rebuke sins so that others would know what was right and wrong, and he was not to share in those sins – i.e. either by doing them or keeping quiet about them. He was to keep himself 'pure' and the Greek, *hagnos*, means chaste, pure, clean, and this may imply that the big problem for the Christians in Ephesus was sexual sins.

Timothy is to keep and carry out all these instructions, without partiality and favouritism. Whoever sinned, friend or acquaintance or stranger, needed to be admonished, reproved. This was so serious that Paul laid a solemn charge on Timothy, before God and the elect angels, but who are the 'elect' angels.

It may be that these angels are described as 'elect' to distinguish them from the 'fallen' angels. Or it may be that these 'elect' angels take part in the last judgment; Matthew 13:41; 25:31; Mark 8:38.

Timothy is also told not to be hasty in laying on of hands. During the period of time covered by the Acts of the Apostles it seems that Jewish Christians needed the Apostles to lay hands on them before they received the Holy Spirit (see Acts 8:14-18; 19:1-7). On the other hand, Gentile Christians of that time received the Spirit when they believed (Acts 10:43-45). However, following the blindness and deafness of the nation of Israel at the end of Acts, and God's salvation being sent to the Gentiles (Acts 28:25-28), Paul wrote the letter to the Ephesians early in the two year imprisonment (Acts 28:30). In that letter we learn that *all* believers now received the Holy Spirit when they believe the gospel of salvation (Ephesians 1:13-14). Thus Paul could not have been referring to the laying on of hands for the receipt of the Holy Spirit.

Another suggestion comes from a practice which was common by the third century; see Eusebius *Church History*, vii, 2. There we read that it became the custom to lay hands on a penitent sinner who had given proof of his repentance. However, there is nothing in the Bible to suggest that this was the situation during New Testament times.

A third explanation is that this was to do with the appointment of elders, deacons, overseers etc. At their ordination, hands were laid on them, signifying that they were the approved appointee. Again, there is nothing in the New Testament that specifically indicates this was the case. However, it does fit the context better than the previous two suggestions. Paul had earlier written to Timothy about appointing overseers and deacons and was told that they should not be a new convert and should be tried and tested (1 Timothy 3:6,10). Hence Timothy should not hastily appoint, lay hands on, anyone.

1 Timothy 5:23: Stop drinking only water, and use a little wine because of your stomach and your frequent illnesses.

This verse may provide an explanation as to why Timothy needed to be encouraged into using his gift of teaching. He was frequently ill with what seems to be stomach problems. This may have affected Timothy in two ways; physically and mentally.

First, anyone who has suffered from frequent illness, and especially if it involves the stomach, knows how debilitating such a condition is, often sapping energy and resulting in lethargy.

However, secondly, Timothy knew that if he had had this condition just a few years earlier, during the time covered by the Acts of the Apostles, even a handkerchief from Paul would have healed him (Acts 19:12). However, following the hardening of their hearts by the nation of Israel such gifts, which were signs to the people of Israel[14], began to cease. Paul did not heal Epaphroditus but, thankfully, he did eventually recover (Philippians 2:25-30). Paul left Trophimus sick at Miletus, but earlier he had left no-one sick on Malta (2 Timothy 4:20; Acts 28:9). Thus Timothy may have felt aggrieved that he was not cured.

1 Timothy 5:24-25: The sins of some men are obvious, reaching the place of judgment ahead of them; the sins of others trail behind them. In the same way, good deeds are obvious, and even those that are not cannot be hidden.

Some sins some people commit openly, brazenly, boastfully. Others, perhaps more serious ones, are done quietly, in secret and, as a result, we may not be aware of such a person's character for quite some time. However, believers in Christ are not concerned with practising sin (1 John 3:9; 5:18), but with doing good deeds. Some of these good deeds should be open and obvious, just as our Lord said when He was talking about his followers being the light of the world.

> "In the same way, let your light shine before men, that they may see your good deeds and praise your Father in heaven." (Matthew 5:16)

Our Lord also spoke of 'acts of righteousness' (*NIV*). These are acts of benevolence, or the giving of alms (*KJV*). Of these He said,

---

[14] For a fuller treatment of how miracles were signs to the people of Israel see *The Miracles of the Apostles* by Michael Penny, published by the Open Bible Trust.

"Be careful not to do your 'acts of righteousness' before men, to be seen by them. If you do, you will have no reward from your Father in heaven." (Matthew 6:1)

Although done in secret, such acts, and other kindnesses done in private, cannot be hidden as often those who benefit will not remain silent.

1 Timothy
Chapter 6

1 Timothy
Chapter 6

1 Timothy 6:1-2: All who are under the yoke of slavery should consider their masters worthy of full respect, so that God's name and our teaching may not be slandered. Those who have believing masters are not to show less respect for them because they are brothers. Instead, they are to serve them even better, because those who benefit from their service are believers, and dear to them. These are the things you are to teach and urge on them.

Paul wrote about the relationship between slaves and masters in Ephesians 6:5-9 and Colossians 3:22-4:1. However, perhaps the most poignant passage comes in Philemon where he, the slave owner, is told to treat the slave, Onesimus, "as a brother" (verse 16).

Some are concerned that slavery was not overtly criticised and condemned in the New Testament. However, if it had been abolished there would have been mass unemployment, poverty and even starvation. Following the teaching given by the Apostle Paul would result in slavery slowly disappearing, which is what happened in those early Christian communities. Sadly it raised its ugly head again, reaching a peak in the 18th and early 19th century, thankfully to be abolished by the actions of the Christian politician, William Wilberforce.

1 Timothy 6: 3-5: If anyone teaches false doctrines and does not agree to the sound instruction of our Lord Jesus Christ

and to godly teaching, he is conceited and understands nothing. He has an unhealthy interest in controversies and quarrels about words that result in envy, strife, malicious talk, evil suspicions and constant friction between men of corrupt mind, who have been robbed of the truth and who think that godliness is a means to financial gain.

What false doctrines were being taught at that time? We have mentioned some of them previously, but we can add to that list.

- Gentiles had to be circumcised to be saved (Acts 15:1);
- Gentiles had to obey the Law of Moses (Acts 15:5);
- There was no resurrection of the dead (1 Corinthians 15:12);
- The resurrection of believers had already taken place (2 Timothy 2:18);
- Christ, as God, did not have a real, human body (1 John 4:2-3; 2 John 7);
- Worshipping angels (Colossians 2:18);
- Forbidding to marry (1 Timothy 4:3);
- Abstaining from food (1 Timothy 4:3).

And as well as doctrinal error, there were those who did not agree with godly teaching which dealt with how people should live. As a result they generated a whole slough of problems resulting in people arguing and bickering and quarrelling, displaying all those shortcomings which grieve the Holy Spirit of God (Ephesians 4:30-31). Such men were corrupt and, somehow or other, thought that godliness was a means to financial gain, a view not uncommon today amongst some who hold to the 'prosperity gospel'. However, Titus was also warned of such people.

For there are many rebellious people, mere talkers and deceivers, especially those of the circumcision group. They must be silenced, because they are ruining whole households by teaching things they ought not to teach— and that for the sake of dishonest gain. (Titus 1:10-11).

The 'circumcision group' were Christian Jews, or Jews who purported to be Christian, and one of the things that they advocated was that Gentiles had to be circumcised to be saved. They were willing to perform the operation, provided they were paid!

1 Timothy 6:6-8: But godliness with contentment is great gain. For we brought nothing into the world, and we can take nothing out of it. But if we have food and clothing, we will be content with that.

Godliness does not bring financial gain, but it should bring contentment. However, that does not come naturally and may take some time, and we often have to learn the truth of it. Even the Apostle Paul wrote, "I have *learned* to be content whatever the circumstances" (Philippians 4:11).

We do not have the 'right' to possessions as we brought nothing into the world and will take nothing out of it. So, let us be content with what we need, food and clothing, and Paul told the Philippians that God would meet all their needs in Christ Jesus, not all their wants (Philippians 4:19).

1 Timothy 6:9-10: People who want to get rich fall into temptation and a trap and into many foolish and harmful desires that plunge men into ruin and destruction. For the love of money is a root of all kinds of evil. Some people, eager

for money, have wandered from the faith and pierced themselves with many griefs.

There is nothing wrong with either riches or money. It is the 'love' of money and the 'desire' for riches which cause all the problems. Such love and such desire can lead people into making unethical decisions, to cut corners, to walk over others. Such behaviour, sooner or later, rebounds upon the person and causes them much grief.

1 Timothy 6:11-12: But you, man of God, flee from all this, and pursue righteousness, godliness, faith, love, endurance and gentleness. Fight the good fight of the faith. Take hold of the eternal life to which you were called when you made your good confession in the presence of many witnesses.

The man of God should not run after riches but rather pursue the fruit of the Spirit, especially faith and love, godliness and gentleness, righteousness and endurance. However, we are saved by grace through faith and have eternal life, and by pursuing the right things the man of God will build up treasure in heaven, the pure treasure that does not corrupt the heart (Matthew 6:19-20) . This is the good fight, and the fight is often against ourselves, against our own selfish desires.

1 Timothy 6:13-16: In the sight of God, who gives life to everything, and of Christ Jesus, who while testifying before Pontius Pilate made the good confession, I charge you to keep this command without spot or blame until the appearing of our Lord Jesus Christ, which God will bring about in his own time - God, the blessed and only Ruler, the King of kings and Lord of lords, who alone is immortal and who lives in

unapproachable light, whom no one has seen or can see. To him be honour and might forever. Amen.

Paul now solemnly charges Timothy, before God and Christ, to keep the command to flee from the desire to get rich and the love of money, and rather to fight the good fight, by pursuing the Christian graces. He wants him to keep it 'without spot or blame'. Other, outsiders, will be watching him and failure to keep this command will bring criticism not only upon him, but also upon the church (the household of God), and the name of Jesus Christ.

And here we have a lovely accolade: God, the blessed and only ruler, the King of kings and Lord of lords, who alone is immortal …. Who alone is immortal? Yes! That is what it says. Satan is not immortal, neither is the archangel Michael, and neither are you and I. However, that is our present position and there will come a day when God is going to share or give His immortality to others (1 Corinthians 15:51-54).

To this God, the one who alone is immortal and who lives in unapproachable light, to Him be honour and might ... forever.

1 Timothy 6:17-19: Command those who are rich in this present world not to be arrogant nor to put their hope in wealth, which is so uncertain, but to put their hope in God, who richly provides us with everything for our enjoyment. Command them to do good, to be rich in good deeds, and to be generous and willing to share. In this way they will lay up treasure for themselves as a firm foundation for the coming age, so that they may take hold of the life that is truly life.

Paul now returns to riches, and he does not say that those who have them should give them all away, but they should use them.

However, he first tells them not to be arrogant, and wealth can so easily bring arrogance, and neither are they to put their hope in wealth, which is so uncertain, as we have seen with the stock market collapse, the bursting of the housing bubble, the recession and low interest rates. No! Nothing is definite in this life, but the hope we have in God is a sure and certain hope. It is the certain hope of forgiveness and eternal life, because it is based not upon me, but is built on the foundation of Jesus Christ's death and resurrection.

> The words "it was credited to him" were written not for him alone, but also for us, to whom God will credit righteousness—for us who believe in him who raised Jesus our Lord from the dead. He was delivered over to death for our sins and was raised to life for our justification. (Romans 4:23-25)

However, those who are fortunate enough to have riches have the privilege of sharing their wealth with others. If they wisely and generously use the wealth they have in this life, they will store up treasure for themselves in heaven for eternal life.

1 Timothy 6:20-21: Timothy, guard what has been entrusted to your care. Turn away from godless chatter and the opposing ideas of what is falsely called knowledge, which some have professed and in so doing have wandered from the faith. Grace be with you.

As usual Paul signs off with a reference to 'grace'. However, before that he has some salutary things to say to Timothy which are equally relevant to us.

Much doctrine and teaching had been entrusted to Timothy, and he was to guard it. We, too, need to guard what has been entrusted to us; the Scriptures and the wonderful gospel of salvation by grace through faith in Christ. The Scriptures are God breathed (2 Timothy 3:16) and are our authority. And there is no other gospel (Galatians 1:6-9).

And Timothy is told to turn away from godless chatter and ideas which are opposed the Christian faith, both of which are very prevalent in our society today. In the 21st century we hear much about *spirituality*, which sounds so good but there is no substance to it. It is just a collection of ideas and is based neither on sound knowledge nor revelation from God.

Appendix 1: The role of women in the church

Appendix 1:
The role of women
in the church

When writing to Timothy Paul gave many instructions concerning prayer, men and women, overseers and deacons. Much of it is non-controversial but one passage has been the source of much debate in Christian circles; that is 1 Timothy 2:11-14.

> A woman should learn in quietness and full submission. I do not permit a woman to teach or to assume authority over a man; she must be quiet. For Adam was formed first, then Eve. And Adam was not the one deceived; it was the woman who was deceived and became a sinner.

Men, women and prayer

Earlier in this letter, Paul had written:

> I want men everywhere to lift up holy hands in prayer, without anger and disputing. (1 Timothy 2:8)

Because of this verse some do not allow women to pray in church, insisting that here the Bible teaches that only men should pray. However, if we look at 1 Corinthians 11:5 we read about women who prayed in the church at Corinth, and if it was permitted in Corinth, then no doubt it was permitted elsewhere.

It is more likely that the instruction in 1 Timothy 2:8 is to the men, telling them they should not pray in meetings if they were angry and had just been in an argument, possibly disputing and debating doctrinal issues.

Women teaching and prophesying

When we read of 'prophecy' our immediate thoughts turn to the future. However, a prophet was someone who spoke about God, saying what God did in the past, what He is doing in the present, or what He will do in the future. Thus a prophet, although not the same as, was not dissimilar to a teacher. In the same passage we noted earlier, 1 Corinthians 11:5, we read of women prophesying, and Phillip had four daughters who were prophetesses (Acts 21:9).

We also read of Priscilla and Aquila teaching Apollos, and *they* "explained to him the way of God more adequately," (Acts18:24-26). Paul described them as "my fellow-workers in Christ Jesus" in Romans 16:3, and we learn that there was a church in their home (1 Corinthians 16:19).

Then, at the end of Romans we read of two of Paul's relatives, Andronicus and Junias who had been in prison with Paul and who were "outstanding among the apostles" (Romans 16:7). Like Saul, who was also called by the Greek equivalent Paul, they had Greek names which may mean that they were from Tarsus like him.

However, *The Companion Bible* note on Junias is ambiguous, stating that the word is in the accusative case and it may indicate 'Junias' (masculine) or 'Junia' (feminine).

Strong, in his *Exhaustive Concordance* indicates that it is 'Junia' and some ancient manuscripts have 'Julia'. If that is the case then we have a female apostle and apostles did prophesy and teach.

From the Old Testament it is clear that Israel's leaders were men, except for Deborah. It is also true that the majority of prophets were men, but there were a number of exceptions: Miriam (Exodus 15:20); Deborah (Judges 4:4); Huldah (2 Kings 22:14; 2 Chronicles 34:22-28).

In the New Testament Anna is called a prophetess (Luke 2:36). However, it is clear from the New Testament that the teachers and prophets were mainly men, but not exclusively and we have mentioned some exceptions.

But why didn't women teach?

In Old Testament times, and in the Judaism of the New Testament, Hebrew fathers had their sons educated in the Scriptures; the Law, the Prophets and the Psalms. They may have done some of this themselves but once the synagogue movement had been developed, the sons were also taught by the rabbi.

However, they did not teach their daughters because that was seen as the prerogative of the girl's future husband. There was great diversity in Judaism but it was essential that there should be unity in the home. Thus it was more important for a woman to agree with her husband's theology than her father's. Thus Jewish women were basically uneducated, and so were in no way equipped to teach anyone.

However, Gentile women, especially those in the Greco-Roman world, could be highly educated, and this may have spread to some of the women of the Jewish dispersion. Priscilla was a Jewess from Rome (Acts 18:1-3) and was clearly an able woman.

As we have mentioned, when we read through the New Testament we see just a few women in prominent positions, but also we should note that there were few, if any, Gentiles in prominent positions; neither Gentile men nor Gentile women Why was that?

> What advantage, then, is there in being a Jew, or what value is there in circumcision? Much in every way! First of all, they [the Jews] have been entrusted with the very words of God. (Romans 3:1-2)

Thus the Jewish Christians had an advantage (at that time) over the Gentile Christians; the Jewish Christians had the Scriptures and knew them; the Gentiles did not. It is not until well past the end of Acts that we see a Gentile, Titus, given a significant leadership role on the island of Crete, and that was some twenty years after he was saved; (see Paul's letter to Titus).

Similarly with the women of that time; most, whether Jewish or Gentile, did not know the Scriptures. Thus they were at a distinct disadvantage and so needed to be taught, rather than teach. However, as we have seen, there were exceptions. There may have been many more women prophets than there were women teachers. A prophet was inspired and enabled by the Holy Spirit to speak, but a teacher needed to know the Scriptures before he / she could explain them.

Women to be silent in the church

In 1 Corinthians 14:33-35 we have another controversial, and in some quarters, misunderstood passage. There we read:

> As in all the congregations of the Lord's people, women should remain silent in the churches. They are not allowed

to speak, but must be in submission, as the law says. If they want to inquire about something, they should ask their own husbands at home; for it is disgraceful for a woman to speak in the church.

This passage has been used to support the idea that women should not preach, pray or say anything in the church. However, such a view is clearly incorrect for we have already read, in 1 Corinthians 11:5, women prayed and prophesied in the Corinthian church.

Some suggest 1 Corinthians 14 is dealing with women talking and chattering, but it is more likely that the women were discussing what was being taught, trying to understand it. Here they are told, and again this is in harmony with what we have said earlier, to ask their own husbands at home.

Woman = wife; man = husband

However, there is another problem with 1 Timothy 2:11-14. Because the Greek word for woman (*gune*) is also the Greek word for wife, and is translated so in many places (e.g. Acts 5:1,2,7; 18:2;24:24; Ephesians 5:23,33). Also the Greek word for man (*aner*) is translated husband in the majority of places (e.g. Acts 5:9,10; Ephesians 5:23,33). Thus this passage could, and probably should, be translated:

> A wife should learn in quietness and full submission. I do not permit a wife to teach or to assume authority over a husband. (See footnotes in the *New Revised Standard Version* and in the 2010 edition of the *New International Version* and notes on 1 Timothy 2:9 in *The Companion Bible.*)

This translation, and its consequential interpretation, is in harmony with what we wrote earlier about the non-education of Jewish daughters and the desire for homes to be a unity so that the woman should be taught by her husband. It is also in harmony with what we read elsewhere in Scripture; for example in 1 Peter 3:1-2:

> Wives, in the same way submit yourselves to your own husbands so that, if any of them do not believe the word, they may be won over without words by the behaviour of their wives, when they see the purity and reverence of your lives.

Peter wrote to the Jewish dispersion scattered over various parts of the world (1 Peter 1:1). Some, in those synagogues, had become Christians but what if a woman believed Jesus to be the Christ, the Messiah, her Saviour, but her husband did not? She was **not** to 'teach' him.

Appendix 2: God wants, wishes, all men to be saved

Appendix 2:
God wants, wishes, all men to be saved

In Christendom, at the moment, there are two opposing ideas. One is that only those who believe in the Lord Jesus Christ have eternal life and the rest of humanity is to suffer eternal torment. The other is that God wishes all men to be saved and is, indeed, the Saviour of all men, as Christ gave Himself as a ransom for all men. Thus, ultimately, everyone who has ever lived will have eternal life.

Both of these views quote passages from the Bible to support their case, and each criticises the other as being unjust. Clearly there are many who have never heard of Jesus, thus to condemn them to an eternity of punishment is hardly righteous. However, to allow people like Hitler, and other despots who have caused untold misery for millions, to live in paradise for eternity is hardly righteous either. However, there is a little known third view.

The Bible speaks of two resurrections. In the words of our Lord Jesus Christ we read:

> "I tell you the truth, whoever hears my word and believes him who sent me has eternal life and will not be condemned; he has crossed over from death to life. I tell you the truth, a time is coming and has now come when the dead will hear the voice of the Son of God and those who hear will live. For as the Father has life in himself, so

he has granted the Son to have life in himself. And he has given him authority to judge because he is the Son of Man." (John 5:24-27)

This resurrection refers to those who 'believe'; i.e. those who are 'saved' and are guaranteed eternal life. These will hear the voice of the Son of God and will be raised to eternal life. However, the Lord then went on to talk of a second resurrection.

"Do not be amazed at this, for a time is coming when all who are in their graves will hear his voice and come out— those who have done good will rise to live, and those who have done evil will rise to be condemned. By myself I can do nothing; I judge only as I hear, and my judgment is just, for I seek not to please myself but him who sent me." (John 5:28-30)

This resurrection refers to the rest of the dead; those who did not 'believe'; those who were not 'saved'; those not raised at the previous resurrection. All these will be raised at this second resurrection and all will be judged by Christ, and his judgments are just. He bases His judgment on what they have done in this life. Those whom He deems to have done good will rise to have eternal life. However, those whom He deems to have done evil will be condemned.

John gives us a similar picture in Revelation 20. There he talks about the first resurrection (Revelation 20:4-6), and then goes on to talk about a second.

Then I saw a great white throne and him who was seated on it. Earth and sky fled from his presence, and there was no place for them. And I saw the dead, great and small, standing before the throne, and books were opened. Another book was opened, which is the book of life. The dead were judged according to what they had done as recorded in the books. The sea gave up the dead that were in it, and death and Hades gave up the dead that were in them, and each person was judged according to what he had done. Then death and Hades were thrown into the lake of fire. The lake of fire is the second death. If anyone's name was not found written in the book of life, he was thrown into the lake of fire. (Revelation 20:11-15)

Here, again, the first resurrection is for those who have followed Christ, but the second deals with "the rest of the dead" (Revelation 20:5). These, again, are judged according to their works and some have their names written in the book of life. Others, however, are condemned, but not to an eternal 'punishing' of suffering, but to an eternal 'punishment'; the second death in the lake of fire.

It may be hard for us to envisage how such a judgment of works can be equitable, but that is not our role, that is Christ's. This was an issue in New Testament times and Paul addressed it in Romans where he indicates that the unbelieving Jew of his time would be judged against the Law of Moses, but the pagans would be judged against the Law of Conscience (Romans 2:12-16). This, again, would be hard, even impossible, for us to do, but God is the Righteous Judge so we should leave it in His hands.

This third understanding does solve many problems; the injustice of eternal torment; the injustice of no eternal life for those who have never heard of Christ; the injustice of giving eternal life to everyone and anyone no matter what atrocities they may have committed.

Difficult verses

There are, of course, difficult verses which may need some explanation. Our English Bibles do have expressions such as "tormented day and night for ever and ever" (Revelation 20:10). However, just a few verses later we read of the creation of a New Heavens and New Earth where there is no more pain and the old order of things has passed away (Revelation 21:4). The expression 'for ever and ever', literally translated from the Greek, would be 'until the age of the ages'. The 'until' tells us such torment is not for ever. The 'age of the ages' is an idiom we well understand in such expressions as King of kings and Lord of lords. Thus the 'age of the ages' is the supreme age, the creation of the New Heavens and New Earth which are the home of righteousness (2 Peter 3:13), and where there is no more mourning, crying or pain (Revelation 21:4).

In the other camp we do have verses which state that "God is the Saviour of all men" (1 Timothy 4:10). It is true that Jesus died for the sins of the whole world and so salvation is available to all people. However, that does not mean all are saved. Care must be taken with seemingly universal words like 'all' or 'everyone' or 'anything'. For example, we read in Matthew 26:31 that our Saviour said, "This very night you will all fall away on account of me". Eleven of them did, but there is no record that John fell away. He followed Christ right into the house of the high priest, and was even there at the foot of the cross (John 18:15-16; 19:25-27).

When we use words like 'all' or 'everyone' we seldom use them with a universal meaning. At the start of a meeting we may ask 'Is everyone here?' or 'Are we all here?' but we do not mean 'everyone in the world'. We mean everyone within a clearly defined subset.

Again, when our Lord told them, "And I will do whatever you ask in my name … You may ask me for anything in my name, and I will do it" (John14:13-14). He was not giving them a blank cheque. Paul prayed for his 'thorn in the flesh' to be removed, but the Lord refused his request (2 Corinthians 12:7-12).

In 1 Corinthians 15:22 we read, "As in Adam all die, so in Christ all will be made alive." Of course not 'all' are going to die, as Paul makes clear later in the chapter when he writes about those who do not die but who are changed when Christ returns (1 Corinthians 15:51-52). And Isaiah told Israel that some will not rise, but that their dead will rise (Isaiah 26:14,19). However, even if some wish to hold the view that 'all' may be raised, we cannot assume that 'all' will be given eternal life. All who believe in Christ will be part of the first resurrection and will have eternal life. However, for those who have a part in the second resurrection, whether or not their names are written in the book of life depends upon Christ's judgement. Some will suffer the second death, as Revelation 20:15 makes clear.

To sum up

The ones who are 'saved' are those who believe (1 Timothy 4:10) because people are saved by grace through faith and not by works (Ephesians 2:8-9). However, those who do not believe in Christ are not saved but have a later resurrection and may or may not be granted eternal life; depending on whether or not Christ judges them to have done well.

Also in this series

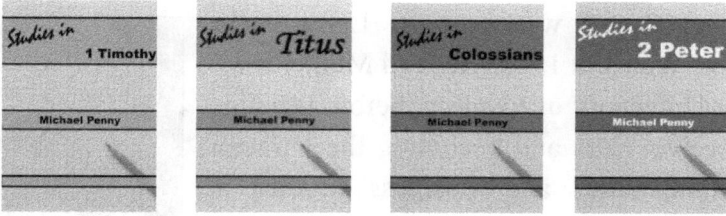

Michael Penny has written, or edited, a number of other books in this series including:

- **Studies in 1 Thessalonians**
- **Studies in 2 Thessalonians**
- **Studies in Colossians**
- **Studies in Philemon**
- **Studies in Philippians**
- **Studies in 1 Timothy**
- **Studies in 2 Timothy**
- **Studies in Titus**
- **Studies in 2 Peter**
- **Studies in John's Epistles**
- **Studies in Jude**
- **Studies in Ruth**

These are also available as eBooks and KDP paperbacks.

Details from www.obt.org.uk

About the author

Michael Penny was born in Ebbw Vale, Gwent, Wales in 1943. He read Mathematics at the University of Reading, before teaching for twelve years and becoming the Director of Mathematics and Business Studies at Queen Mary's College Basingstoke in Hampshire, England. In 1978 he entered Christian publishing, and in 1984 became the administrator of The Open Bible Trust.

He held this position for seven years, before moving to the USA and becoming pastor of Grace Church in New Berlin, Wisconsin. He returned to Britain in 1999, and is at present the Administrator and Editor of The Open Bible Trust. From 2010 he has been Chairman of Churches Together in Reading, where he speaks in a number of churches of different denominations. He is also a member of the Advisory Committee to Reading University Christian Union and a chaplain at Reading College.

He is lead chaplain for Activate Learning and has set up chaplaincy teams in a number of their colleges including Reading College, The City of Oxford College, Bracknell and Wokingham College, and Blackbird Leys College.

He lives near Reading with his wife and has appeared on Premier Radio and BBC Radio Berkshire many times. He has made several speaking tours of America, Canada, Australia, New Zealand and the Netherlands, as well as others to South Africa and the Philippines. Some of his writings have been translated into German and Russian.

Also by Michael Penny

He has written many books including:

40 Problem Passages,
Galatians: Interpretation and Application,
Joel's Prophecy: Past and Future,
Approaching the Bible,
The Miracles of the Apostles,
The Manual on the Gospel of John
The Bible! Myth or Message?

Plus two written with W M Henry:

The Will of God: Past and Present
Following Philippians
Abraham and his seed (with chapters by Sylvia Penny also)

His latest three books are:

James: His life and letter
Peter: His life and letters.
Paul: A Missionary of Genius

Further details of all these books can be seen on

www.obt.org.uk

from where they can also be ordered.

They are also available as eBooks from Amazon and Apple and
as KDP paperbacks from Amazon.

Further details of the books on these pages
can be seen on

www.obt.org.uk

The books are available from that website and from

The Open Bible Trust
Fordland Mount, Upper Basildon,
Reading, RG8 8LU, UK.

They are also available as eBooks from Amazon and
Apple and as
KDP paperback from Amazon

Further reading

The Miracles of the Apostles

Michael Penny

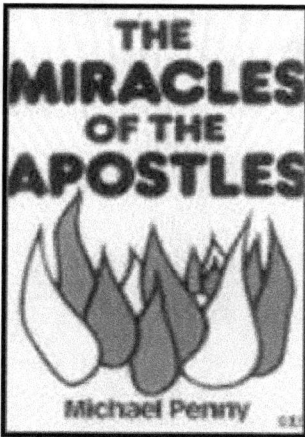

Why did the Apostles perform miracles?
Why were they able to perform them?
What was the purpose of the miracles?
What did they signify to the Jews?
Why did the Gentiles misunderstand them?
Why was Paul, later, not able to heal?
When did the miracles cease?
Why did they cease?

This book answers these questions, explains the significance and purpose of each type of miracle performed by the Apostles, and makes it clear why such miracles are not in evidence today.

Salvation

Safe and Secure
Sylvia Penny

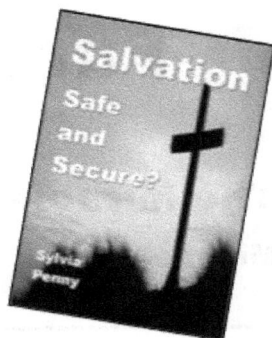

This important book is a thorough treatment of the subject of salvation, asking such questions as ...

- What is it, exactly, that saves us?
- Is salvation secure?
- Can it be lost?
- What is 'conditional security'?

It deals with a wide number of issues such as ...

- Salvation and works
- The doctrine of rewards
- Lordship salvation
- Free grace theology
- Assurance of salvation
- Why people lose their faith

Search magazine

Michael Penny is editor of *Search* magazine.

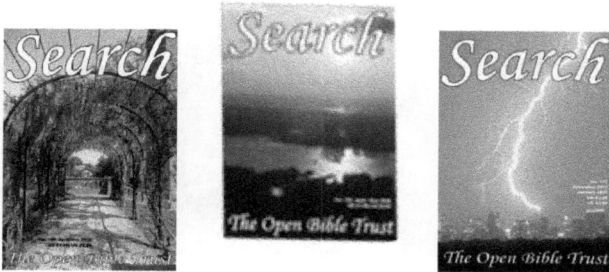

For a free sample of
the Open Bible Trust's magazine *Search*,
please email

admin@obt.org.uk

or visit

www.obt.org.uk/search

About this book

Studies in 1 Timothy

After 2 years of house arrest in Rome (Acts 28:30) Paul embarked on another missionary journey. However, he found Timothy unwell with stomach problems and frequently ill, and seemingly not as enthusiastic for his faith as he once was.

This letter is a loving letter, encouraging Timothy and warning him of false teachers. Paul also gives him advice about a wide range of topics including worship, the appointment of leaders, money and right relationships between people. As such there is much in this letter so relevant to 21st century Christians.

www.ingramcontent.com/pod-product-compliance
Lightning Source LLC
Chambersburg PA
CBHW070537030426
42337CB00016B/2236